THIS WALKER BOOK BELONGS TO:

**Spotted
seahorse**
(Hippocampus kuda)

Dwarf seahorse
(Hippocampus zosterae)

**Short-snouted
seahorse**
*(Hippocampus
hippocampus)*

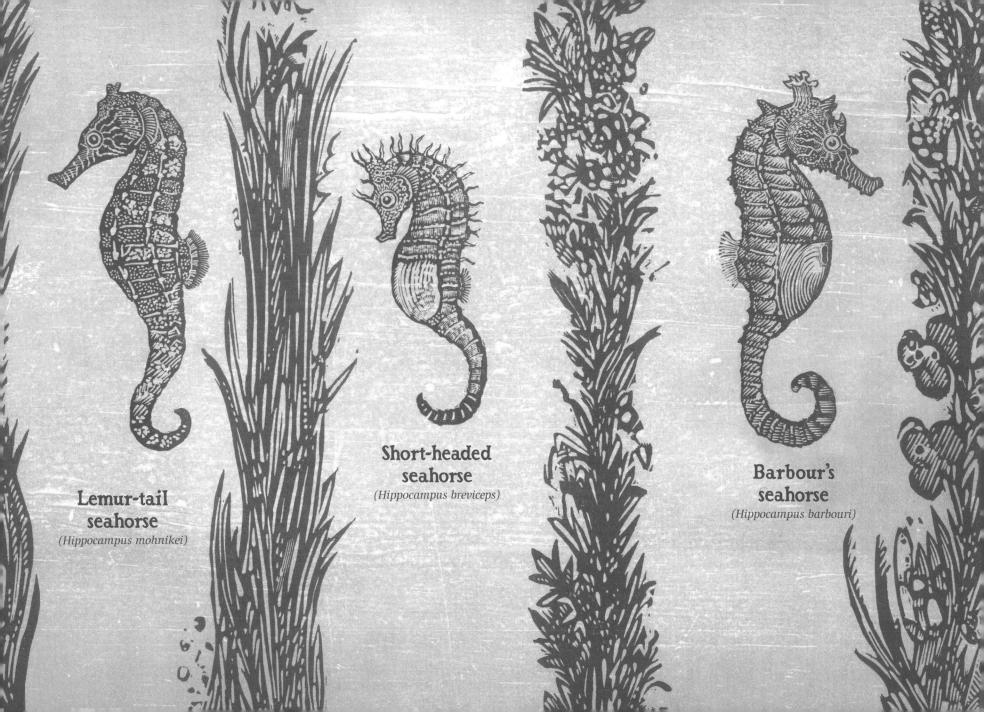

**Lemur-tail
seahorse**
(Hippocampus mohnikei)

**Short-headed
seahorse**
(Hippocampus breviceps)

**Barbour's
seahorse**
(Hippocampus barbouri)

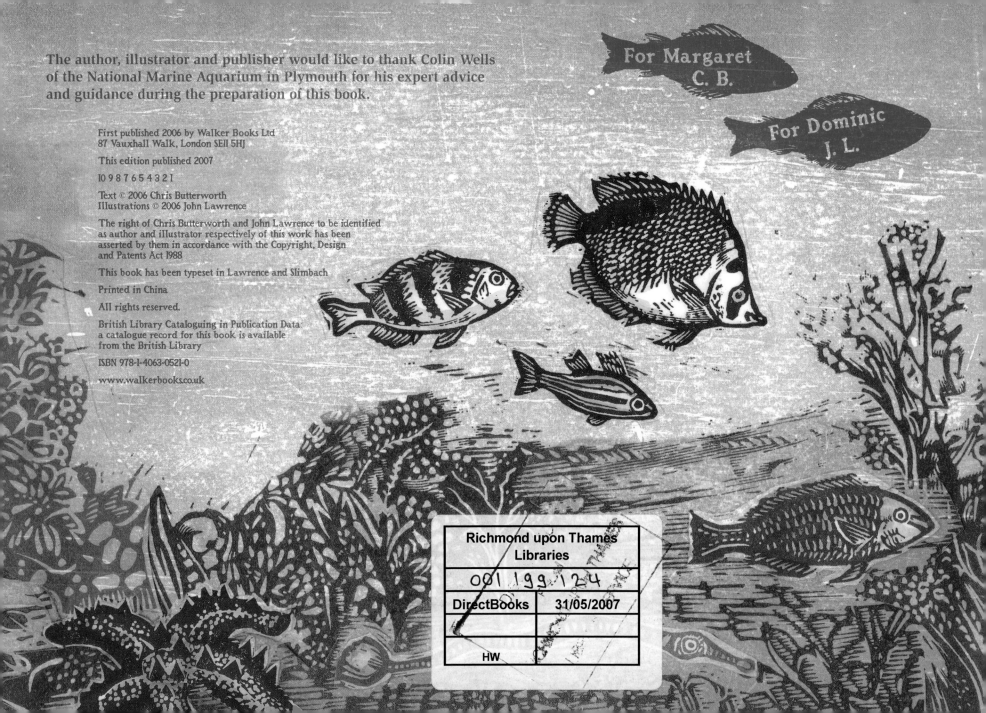

The author, illustrator and publisher would like to thank Colin Wells
of the National Marine Aquarium in Plymouth for his expert advice
and guidance during the preparation of this book.

First published 2006 by Walker Books Ltd
87 Vauxhall Walk, London SE11 5HJ

This edition published 2007

10 9 8 7 6 5 4 3 2 1

Text © 2006 Chris Butterworth
Illustrations © 2006 John Lawrence

The right of Chris Butterworth and John Lawrence to be identified
as author and illustrator respectively of this work has been
asserted by them in accordance with the Copyright, Design
and Patents Act 1988

This book has been typeset in Lawrence and Slimbach

Printed in China

British Library Cataloguing in Publication Data
a catalogue record for this book is available
from the British Library

ISBN 978-1-4063-0521-0

www.walkerbooks.co.uk

For Margaret
C. B.

For Dominic
J. L.

SEAHORSE
The Shyest Fish in the Sea

Chris Butterworth

illustrated by
John Lawrence

WALKER BOOKS
AND SUBSIDIARIES
LONDON · BOSTON · SYDNEY · AUCKLAND

In the warm ocean,
among the waving sea grass meadows,
an eye like a small black bead
is watching the fish dart by.
Who does it belong to?

SEAHORSE –
one of the shyest fish in the sea.

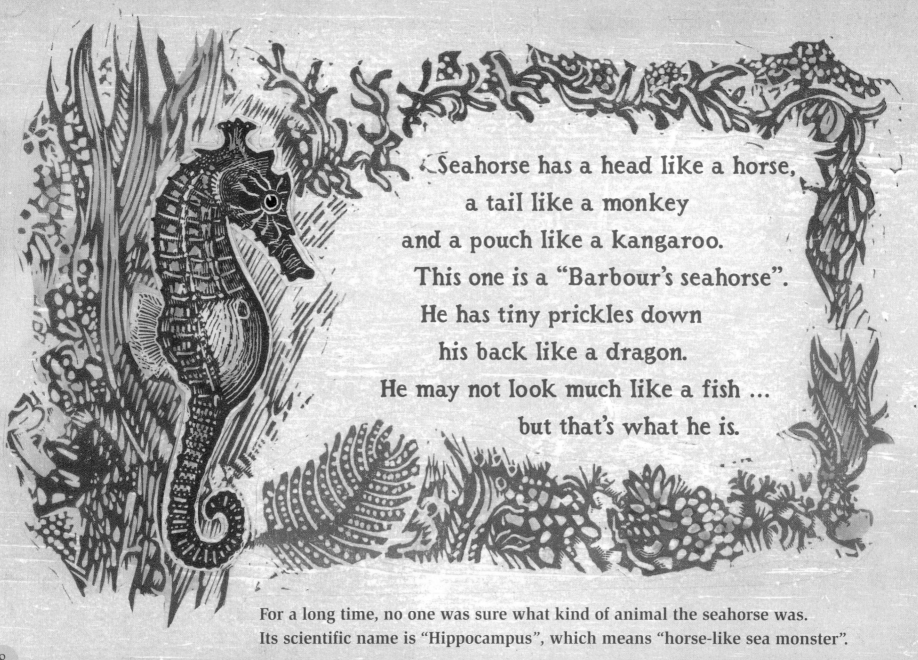

Seahorse has a head like a horse,
a tail like a monkey
and a pouch like a kangaroo.
This one is a "Barbour's seahorse".
He has tiny prickles down
his back like a dragon.
He may not look much like a fish …
but that's what he is.

For a long time, no one was sure what kind of animal the seahorse was.
Its scientific name is "Hippocampus", which means "horse-like sea monster".

Seahorse
swims upright.
He moves himself
through the water
with little fins
on his head,
and a larger one
on his back.

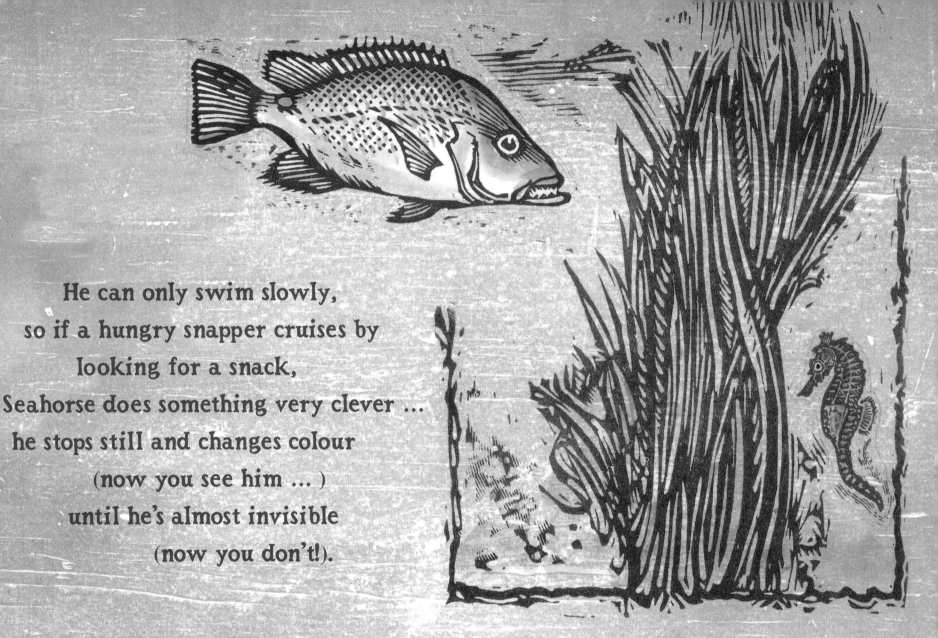

He can only swim slowly,
so if a hungry snapper cruises by
looking for a snack,
Seahorse does something very clever ...
he stops still and changes colour
(now you see him ...)
until he's almost invisible
(now you don't!).

The way seahorses change the colour of their skin

Seahorses have hard bony ridges all down their bodies. Not many other creatures eat them – probably because they're just too difficult to swallow.

to blend in with their surroundings

is called "camouflage".

Every day at sunrise, Seahorse
swims slowly off to meet his mate.
They twist their tails together
and twirl gently round,
changing colour until they match.

Seahorses are faithful to one mate
and often pair up for life.

Today Seahorse's mate is full of ripe eggs.
The two of them dance till sunset,
and then she puts her eggs into his pouch.

Barbour's seahorses mate every few weeks
in the breeding season.

Only male seahorses have a pouch.
Only female seahorses can grow eggs.

Seahorses are the only
male fish to get "pregnant"
like this, growing the young
inside their own bodies.

Seahorse sways about
to get the eggs settled in,
then seals his pouch tight shut.

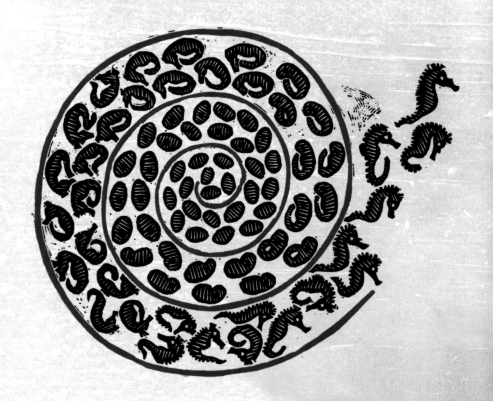

Safe inside, the dots in the eggs
begin to grow into baby seahorses.
They break out of their eggs and go on
growing, every one with a head like a
tiny horse and a tail like a tiny monkey.

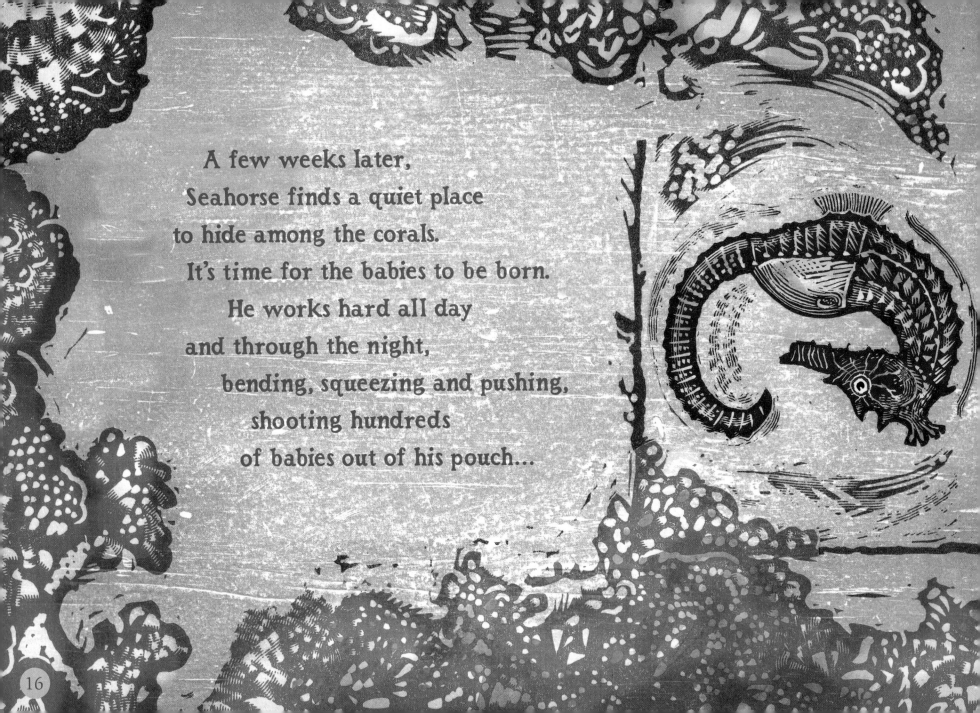

A few weeks later,
Seahorse finds a quiet place
to hide among the corals.
It's time for the babies to be born.
He works hard all day
and through the night,
bending, squeezing and pushing,
shooting hundreds
of babies out of his pouch...

Barbour's seahorses can have two to three hundred babies at one time.

They swirl round him
in the water like smoke.

One or two of the babies hang on to Dad's nose
for a bit (it's the first and biggest thing
they've seen), but when they let go ...

Each tiny new seahorse is a perfect copy of its parents and is ready for life on its own as soon as it's born.

they are so tiny and light that the current soon floats them away.

This new seahorse is only
as long as your eyelash,
but she can find
her own food straight away.
Her eyes move separately
from each other
(one can peer up
while the other looks down)
so she can spot food
coming from any direction.

Seahorses live on "plankton

tiny creatures that float along with the current.

With one quick slurp she sucks
her catch into the end of her snout
and swallows it whole –
seahorses don't have teeth.

To drop lower
in the water,
seahorses
tuck in
their necks
and roll up
their tails.

To rise higher,
they uncurl
themselves
till they
are almost
as straight
as pencils.

When she is big enough,
Seahorse curls up her tail
and sinks down
to the sea bed.

Seahorses can't live where the currents are very strong. They would be swept away.

Here she is safer. Her camouflage protects her, and if a storm scoops
the sea into huge waves or passing boats send the currents sweeping by,
there are plenty of things to hang on to.

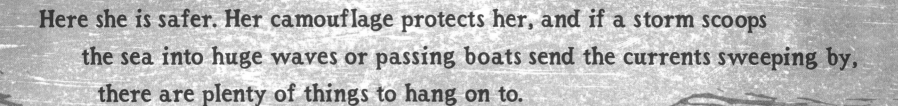

Seahorses have
"prehensile" tails,
which means
they can grasp
things tightly
with them.

23

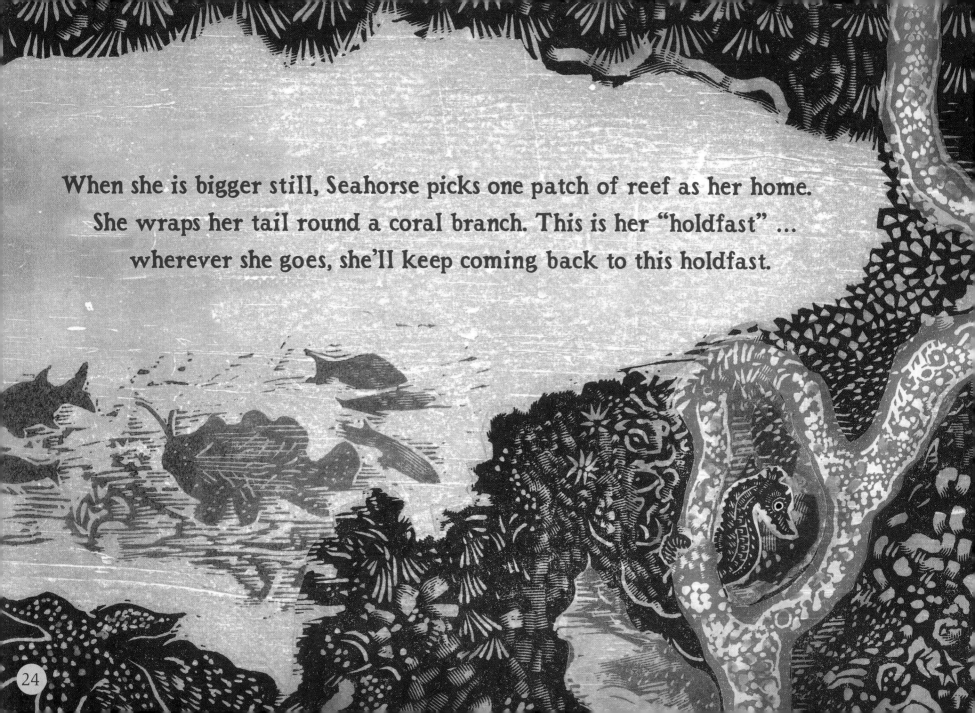

When she is bigger still, Seahorse picks one patch of reef as her home. She wraps her tail round a coral branch. This is her "holdfast" ... wherever she goes, she'll keep coming back to this holdfast.

Male Barbour's seahorses
only range over
a few square metres.
The females' range
is twice as big,
or even bigger.

In a few months
this little seahorse
will be ready to mate.
She'll spend the rest of her life
on the reef, watching for food,
meeting her mate and trying
to stay almost invisible...

Barbour's seahorses can mate
by six months and are
fully grown at about a year.

Who's that peering
from the coral?

Shhhh, she's a seahorse.

Index

Look up the pages to find out about all these seahorse things.

Don't forget to look at both kinds of word – **this kind** and this kind.

About seahorses

The seahorses in this book are Barbour's seahorses, and you can see other kinds of seahorses on the pages at either end of the book. Marine zoologists think there are 35 species, but they may still find others. Many kinds of seahorses need protecting – millions die each year when they are taken from the seas to be sold, and when humans disturb the quiet waters where they live.

About the author

Chris Butterworth loves the sea and the amazing things that live in it. "A seahorse looks as magical as a mermaid," she says, "but while mermaids are made up, seahorses really exist. We need to know as much as we can about them, so we can protect them better. Otherwise one day seahorses might join the mermaids and only exist in stories."

About the illustrator

John Lawrence was born by the sea and has always loved swimming and pottering along the shore. "I never met any seahorses," he says, "so this book has given me the opportunity I missed. They are really exciting to draw and I have tried to imagine how it must be to live under the water like them."

Pacific seahorse
(Hippocampus ingens)

Thorny seahorse
(Hippocampus histrix)

Pygmy seahorse
(Hippocampus bargibanti)

**Zebra
seahorse**
(Hippocampus zebra)

**Long-snouted
seahorse**
(Hippocampus guttulatus)

**Great
seahorse**
(Hippocampus kelloggi)

WALKER BOOKS is the world's leading independent
publisher of children's books. Working with
the best authors and illustrators we create books
for all ages, from babies to teenagers – books your child
will grow up with and always remember. So…

FOR THE BEST CHILDREN'S BOOKS, LOOK FOR THE BEAR